**ANALYZE THE TEXT**

**Author's Purpose** Why do you think the author writes as if you are really blasting off to the Moon?

10, 9, 8, 7, 6, 5, 4, 3, 2, 1 . . . BLAST OFF!

# The Flight

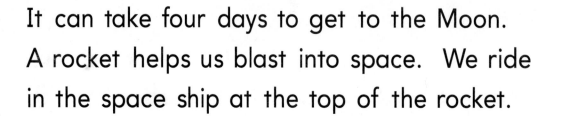

It can take four days to get to the Moon.
A rocket helps us blast into space. We ride
in the space ship at the top of the rocket.

The surface of the Moon is
dusty and has many craters.

There are no plants or animals on the Moon.
There is no water or air.  The Moon has rocks,
dust, and craters.  A crater is a big hole.

# Space Suits

This is astronaut Ronald Evans wearing his space suit.

It's time to put on our space suits. Space suits help keep our skin safe from the very hot sun and the very cold shade.

The space suits have air in them so we can breathe. Now we are dressed for our walk on the Moon.

# Moon Walk

Walking on the Moon is fun.
We can take big, light steps.

**ANALYZE THE TEXT**

**Main Idea and Details** What is the main idea of the section called Moon Walk?

We are very light because the Moon has less gravity than Earth.

23

We carry space tools with us.
We have jobs to do here.

# Moon Rocks

We find rocks and bits of dust to bring back home. We will show the rocks to people back on Earth.

# Lunar Rover

We drive around in our lunar rover. It's even more fun than walking in our fat space suits. Look at all the dust the lunar rover kicks up!

27

# Taking Pictures

We take pictures of our footprints.

We take a picture of our space ship, too.

Our flag is up!

Let's take one last look before we go. We see rocks and dust.

It's time to go back home.

What is it like to be on the Moon?
It's strange and fun at the same time.

When you look up and see the Moon, what do you think? Our Moon is beautiful!

# Dig Deeper

Read Together

## Use Clues to Analyze the Text

Use these pages to learn about Main Idea and Details and Author's Purpose. Then read **Let's Go to the Moon!** again.

## Main Idea and Details

The **topic** is the one big idea that a whole selection is about. Think about the topic in **Let's Go to the Moon!** What is the **main idea**, or the most important idea, about the topic? **Details** are important facts about the main idea. Show the main idea and details on a web.

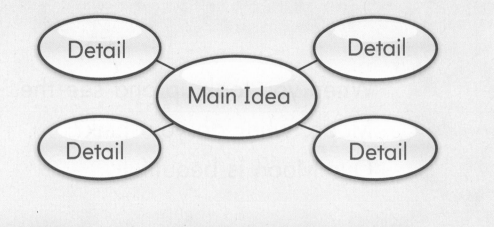

## Author's Purpose

Authors write for many reasons or purposes. They can write to make a reader laugh. They may write to teach the reader about a topic.

Think about what you learned in **Let's Go to the Moon!** Why do you think the author wrote the selection? As you read, find details and text evidence that help to show his purpose.

# Your Turn

 **Turn and Talk**

**What do astronauts do?** Use new words you learned from the selection to describe the different jobs astronauts do. Give details to tell why you think each job is important. Explain your ideas clearly.

## Classroom Conversation

Now talk about these questions with your class.

1 How is the Moon different from Earth?

2 What do astronauts bring to the Moon?

3 Would you like to be an astronaut? Why or why not? Give reasons.

**WRITE ABOUT READING** ································

**Response** Think about what you learned about going to the Moon. What if you could meet the author of this selection? Write four questions you would like to ask him.

### Writing Tip

Begin each question with a capital letter. End it with a question mark.

Read Together

Mae Jemison

A **biography** is a true story about events in a real person's life.

A **time line** shows the order of events. Use the time line on page 42 to retell in order the important events in Mae Jemison's life.

# Mae Jemison

by Debbie O'Brien

Mae Jemison was born in Alabama. Mae knew she wanted to be a scientist when she grew up.

Mae studied very hard in college and became a doctor. She went to Africa because she wanted to help sick people there.

**Here is Mae Jemison on the space shuttle. ▶**

Later, Mae became an astronaut. She had to learn many things before she could go into space.

At last, Mae was ready to fly in the space shuttle. The astronauts had to bring equipment with them. They had to carry food, too. Mae could move around easily in space. She felt light as a feather.

Now Mae has her own company. She wants people to think about science. She tries to show people how science helps them every day.

Mae becomes a doctor.

Mae starts her company.

**1980 1981**          **1987**          **1993**          **1995**

Mae becomes an astronaut.

# Compare Texts

Read Together

## TEXT TO TEXT

**Compare Selections** List ideas and information that are alike in **Mae Jemison** and **Let's Go to the Moon!**

## TEXT TO SELF

**Tell Main Ideas** Tell a partner the most important things you learned about being an astronaut. Use text evidence to explain your ideas clearly.

## TEXT TO WORLD

**Draw and Share** Find a picture of a real planet. Pretend that you have gone there. Draw a picture of things you discovered. Tell about the planet.

# Grammar

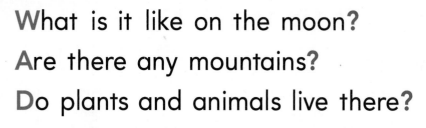

**Questions** A sentence that asks something is called a **question.** A question always begins with a capital letter and ends with a question mark.

Read Together

Digital Resources

▶ Multimedia
Grammar Glossary

> What is it like on the moon?
> Are there any mountains?
> Do plants and animals live there?

44

Write each question correctly.  Use another
sheet of paper.

1. what do astronauts do on the moon

2. do they wear space suits

3. can they jump really far

4. does their buggy go fast

5. why do they take pictures

## Connect Grammar to Writing

When you revise your writing, try using
some questions.

# Narrative Writing

Read Together

✓ **Purpose** When you are writing **sentences about yourself,** be sure all your sentences are about one main idea.

Kim wrote about a cave she saw. Later, she took out a sentence that didn't belong.

**Revised Draft**

My family and I found a cave.

It was very dark inside.

~~I like the woods.~~

**Writing Checklist**

✓ **Purpose** Do all my sentences tell about one main idea?

✓ Does each sentence begin with a capital letter?

✓ Does each sentence end with the correct mark?

Look for the main idea in Kim's final copy. Then revise your writing. Use the Checklist.

**Final Copy**

# A Big Surprise

My family and I found a cave.

It was very dark inside.

We had a big surprise when some bats flew out!

We'll always remember that day.

**Q LANGUAGE DETECTIVE**

**Talk About Words**
Work with a partner.
Read the sentences on
the **Context Cards.**
Turn two of the
sentences into just
one sentence. Make
sure it is a complete
sentence.

# Words to Know

Read Together

▶ Read each **Context Card.**

▶ Make up a new sentence
that uses a blue word.

**1** **there**

There are many ways
to travel safely.

**2** **by**

Wear a helmet when
traveling by bike.

**3** **sure**

Be sure to buckle your seat belt!

**4** **could**

You could walk to the bus with a buddy.

**5** **don't**

Don't stand while the school bus is moving.

**6** **car**

A car should always stop at a STOP sign.

**7** **about**

These children know about bike safety.

**8** **maybe**

Maybe you can help someone be safe.

# Read and Comprehend

## ☑ TARGET SKILL

**Compare and Contrast** How are the characters in a story alike? How are they different? Good readers **compare** and **contrast** characters to understand what they are like and why they act as they do. You can use a diagram to **compare** and **contrast** characters or ideas in a story.

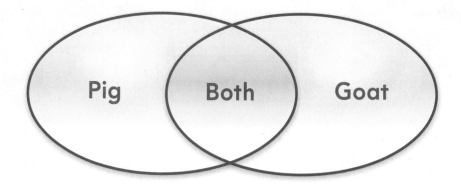

Pig        Both        Goat

## ☑ TARGET STRATEGY

**Visualize** To understand a story, picture in your mind what is happening as you read.

## Ways to Travel

How can you get from one place to another? You could go by car. You could take a train. You could ride a bike. You could run, hop, or skip. You will read about traveling in **The Big Trip.**

### 💬 Talk About It

What do you know about traveling? Think about it. Complete the sentences. Talk about your ideas.

I know ____. I would like to know more about ____.

# ANCHOR TEXT

The Big Trip

VALERI GORBACHEV

## ✅ GENRE

A **fantasy** is a story that could not happen in real life. As you read, look for:
- events that could not really happen
- animals who act like people

**Meet the Author and Illustrator**

## Valeri Gorbachev

Valeri Gorbachev says, "I love to draw for children and to create books when I am both author and illustrator." He also illustrates books for many other authors. To read more about Pig and Goat, look for **Where Is the Apple Pie?** and **One Rainy Day**.

# The Big Trip

### by
## VALERI GORBACHEV

"I am going to take a trip far away,"
Pig said to Goat one day.
"How will you go?" asked Goat.

"Let me think for a moment," said Pig. "Maybe I will go by bike—that will be a very nice trip."

"Oh, dear," said Goat. "You could fall off a bike."

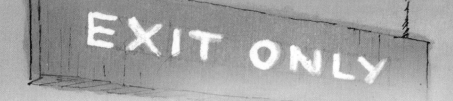

"Ah," said Pig.  "Then I will drive a car."

"It's not a good idea, Pig," said Goat.
"A car can break down!"

**ANALYZE THE TEXT**

**Compare and Contrast** How do Pig and Goat each feel about taking a trip by car?

"Oh," said Pig.  "Then I will
go by horse on my trip."

"I'm not sure about that," said Goat.
"Horses can be very jumpy!"

"Okay," said Pig.  "Then I am going to
go by donkey cart—a donkey is very quiet."

"Not good, not good," said Goat.
"Donkeys can be very stubborn!"

"Then I will go by train," said Pig.

"Oh, Pig, oh, Pig," said Goat,
"a train could get stuck in a tunnel!"

"Good point, Goat," said Pig.
"Then I will fly by plane."

"What if the engine stops!" said Goat.
"You'd have to parachute."

"True," said Pig. "Then I will go by
hot air balloon."

"The hot air balloon could have a hole!" said Goat.

"Okay. I will not travel by land. I will not travel by air. I will go by sea," said Pig. "On a ship."

**ANALYZE THE TEXT**

**Dialogue** How do you know Goat and Pig are speaking? What do they say?

65

"Oh, no!" exclaimed Goat. "Don't do it! The ship could run into a reef when passing through fog."

"Or run into a heavy storm at sea, and there are sharks all around at sea, so many, you couldn't count them!"

"And you could find yourself alone on a desert island in the middle of the ocean with pirates that could come on that desert island by pirate ship!"

"Stop!

# Stop! STOP!"

exclaimed Pig.

"I could fall off a bike
break down in a car
get thrown by a horse
never get there with a donkey
or get stuck on a train.
I might have to parachute from a plane
or from a hot air balloon
and traveling by ship could bring
me many troubles!"

"So, I will not go anywhere," said Pig. "Having a big trip is a very scary thing."

"Unless . . . ," said Goat, looking at Pig,

"you go with a friend."

# Dig Deeper

## Use Clues to Analyze the Text

Use these pages to learn about
Comparing and Contrasting and
Dialogue. Then read **The Big Trip** again.

### Compare and Contrast

Goat and Pig are characters in **The Big
Trip.** How are Pig and Goat different?
How are they alike? You can use a
diagram like this to **compare** and
**contrast** things about Pig and Goat.
Think about their feelings about travel,
their actions, and their ideas.

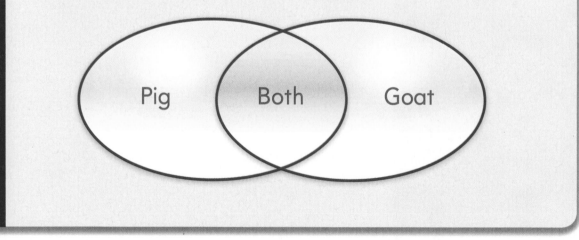

## Dialogue

The words a character says are called **dialogue.** **Quotation marks** go around the words. The word **said** can show who is talking. Writers use dialogue to show what characters say, think, and feel.

You can tell by the dialogue that Pig and Goat take turns telling the story. As you read, think about who is talking and how the characters would say the words.

# Your Turn

## RETURN TO THE ESSENTIAL QUESTION

**Turn and Talk**

**What are some different ways to travel?** What are some ways Pig and Goat talk about in the story? Choose two ways to travel. Take turns with a partner describing one clearly and acting it out.

### 💬 Classroom Conversation

Now talk about these questions with your class.

1 How are Goat and Pig different? How are they alike?

2 What problem do Pig and Goat have? How do they solve it?

3 Which way to travel would you choose?

## WRITE ABOUT READING

**Response** Do you think Pig should travel by car or by bike? Write a sentence to tell which way you think is best for Pig. Write more sentences to give reasons why. Use text evidence to help you explain your ideas.

### Writing Tip

Use **because** and **so** to show how your opinion and reasons go together.

# INFORMATIONAL TEXT

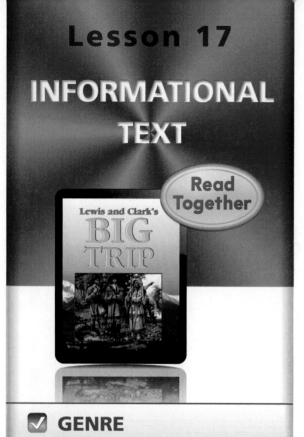

Read Together

# Lewis and Clark's BIG TRIP

Meriwether Lewis and William Clark were explorers who traveled across North America many years ago. They walked, rode horses, and traveled by boat. They wrote about their trip in journals.

Lewis

Clark

Lewis and Clark asked an American Indian named Sacagawea to go with them. The explorers were sure she could help them talk with other American Indians on the way.

One day they came to an American Indian village. Maybe Sacagawea could speak with the people there. She did, and they gave the explorers supplies and horses.

Sacagawea helps Lewis and Clark.

Sacagawea knew good paths across mountains and through forests. It took the explorers about two years to finish their trip. People can travel the same route today by car.

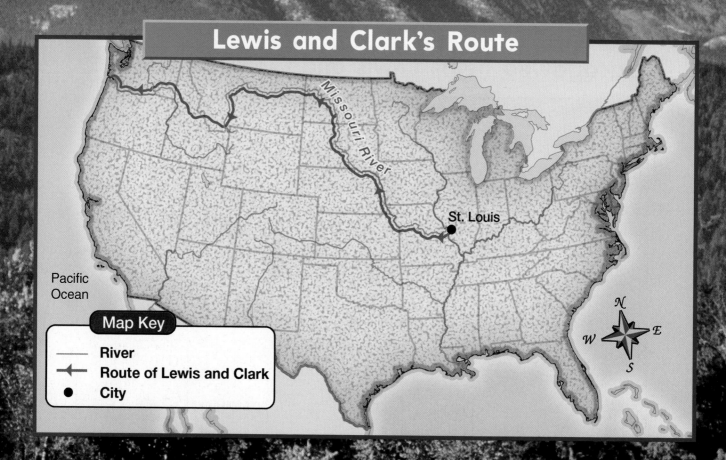

**Lewis and Clark's Route**

Missouri River

St. Louis

Pacific Ocean

Map Key

—— River
← Route of Lewis and Clark
● City

N
W E
S

# Compare Texts

The Big Trip · VALERI GORBACHEV

Lewis and Clark's BIG TRIP

**Read Together**

## TEXT TO TEXT

**Compare Trips** Both selections tell about trips. Tell how the trips are the same and different. Fill in a diagram with a partner.

The Big Trip · Both · Lewis and Clark's Big Trip

## TEXT TO SELF

**Write About a Trip** Write sentences to tell about a trip you took. Tell what happened first, next, and last.

## TEXT TO WORLD

**Learn About the Past** What information did you read in **Lewis and Clark's Big Trip**? What did you learn from the pictures and map?

# Grammar

Digital Resources

▶ Multimedia
Grammar Glossary

Compound Sentences **Compound sentences** are made up of two shorter sentences. The two sentences are connected by words such as **and**, **or**, and **but**.

Read Together

| Compound Sentences | | |
| --- | --- | --- |
| Sentence | Connecting Word | Sentence |
| Pig got on a train, | **and** | he went to the next town. |
| Is it fast, | **or** | is it slow? |
| The trip was long, | **but** | it was lots of fun. |

82

Read aloud each sentence with a partner. Decide if it is a compound sentence. Then write each compound sentence on a sheet of paper. Underline the two short sentences.

1. Pig got a map, and Goat helped him read it.

2. Is the bus on time, or is it late?

3. Pig and Goat ate a snack.

4. Pack your backpack, and bring the map.

5. They will take a train or a bus.

6. I like cars, but planes are faster.

## Connect Grammar to Writing

When you revise your writing, use some compound sentences to make your writing more interesting.

# Narrative Writing

**✓ Development** When you write **sentences about yourself,** help readers picture what you did.  Use details that tell where and when.

Sam wrote about a trip he took.  Later, he added words that tell where he was.

**Revised Draft**

My family went camping.

by a lake

We set up our new tent.
∧

## Writing Checklist

**✓ Development** Do my sentences have details that tell where and when?

✓ Did I write clear letters and use a space between words?

✓ Does each sentence end with the correct mark?

84

Look in Sam's final copy for words that tell where and when. Then revise your own writing. Use the Checklist.

**Final Copy**

# Our Camping Trip

My family went camping.

First, we set up our new tent by a lake.

The next day I was so happy because we rode in a canoe!

It was a great trip.

🔍 **LANGUAGE DETECTIVE**

**Talk About Words**
Work with a partner. Choose one of the **Context Cards.** Add words to the sentence to tell more about the photo. Use details that tell where and when.

# Words to Know

Read Together

▶ Read each **Context Card.**

▶ Ask a question that uses one of the blue words.

**1** **food**

All kinds of food can grow in a garden.

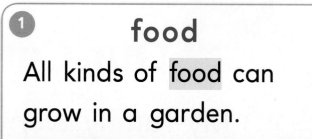

**2** **first**

The seeds are planted in the soil first.

### 3 ground

Keep the ground near the plants wet.

### 4 sometimes

Sometimes pumpkins grow very big!

### 5 under

Carrots grow under the ground.

### 6 these

These tomatoes are ready to be picked.

### 7 right

You can pick pea pods right off of the vine.

### 8 your

What will you plant in your garden?

# Read and Comprehend

✅ **TARGET SKILL**

**Author's Purpose** Authors may write to make you laugh or to give information. The reason an author writes something is called the **author's purpose.** As you read informational text, think about what the author wants you to learn. You can list details that explain the purpose in a chart like this one.

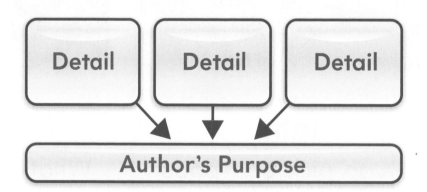

✅ **TARGET STRATEGY**

**Summarize** Stop to tell important ideas about the topic. Use text evidence.

## Agriculture

Many fruits and vegetables grow on farms. First, farmers plant seeds. They take care of the plants. Farmers pick the fruits and vegetables when they are ripe. Then the food is sent to stores for us to buy. You will learn more about food in **Where Does Food Come From?**

### 💬 Think | Write | Pair | Share

What can you see at a farm? Complete the sentence: I can see ___ at a farm. Share with a partner. Act it out.

- ▸ Take turns speaking.
- ▸ Listen carefully.
- ▸ Ask questions.
- ▸ Answer questions.

# ANCHOR TEXT

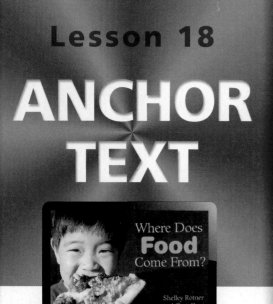

✓ **GENRE**

**Informational text** gives facts about a topic. Look for:

▶ information and facts in the words

▶ photographs that show details about the real world

**Meet the Author and Photographer**

## Shelley Rotner

Shelley Rotner started writing books about things that interested her daughter. If you have questions about the world around you, the answers might be in a book by Ms. Rotner!

**Meet the Author**

## Gary Goss

Gary Goss says, "I love food and creating. I also love working with kids." Mr. Goss has written a children's cookbook called **Blue Moon Soup**.

# Where Does **Food** Come From?

written by
Shelley Rotner
and
Gary Goss

photographs by
Shelley Rotner

**ESSENTIAL QUESTION**

What do farmers need
to grow food?

Cocoa beans are seeds.
They grow on cocoa trees.
Chocolate is made by crushing
and cooking cocoa beans.
Hot cocoa is made from chocolate.

Apples are fruits that grow on trees.
An apple is picked right off the tree.
Apple juice is made by pressing the
juice from apples.

Potatoes are vegetables.
These vegetables grow under the ground.
French fries are made from potatoes.

Wheat is a grain that grows in fields.
Flour can be made by crushing the wheat.
Bread is made from flour.

Rice is a grain.

It grows in wet fields called paddies.

Rice that you eat is made by cooking the grain.

Corn is grain that grows in fields.
Popcorn is made from corn.
First you heat it, and then it pops.

**ANALYZE THE TEXT**

**Conclusions** Do the children like the food they are eating? How can you tell?

Milk comes from cows—
or sometimes from goats.
Butter, cheese, and ice
cream are made from milk.

The eggs you eat are laid by hens.
The hens live on farms.
There are many ways to cook eggs.

Tomatoes grow on vines. Ketchup is made from tomatoes.

**ANALYZE THE TEXT**

**Author's Purpose** Why do the authors show a picture of ketchup near tomatoes?

Honey is made by bees.
They bring the nectar of flowers to the hive.

Maple syrup is made from sap.
The sap drips from maple trees.

Where does your favorite food come from?

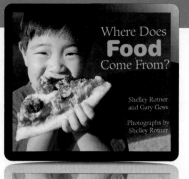

# Dig Deeper

## Use Clues to Analyze the Text

Use these pages to learn about Author's Purpose and Conclusions. Then read **Where Does Food Come From?** again.

### Author's Purpose

Authors write for many reasons. Why do you think the authors wrote **Where Does Food Come From?** What did they want you to learn? You can find details in the selection that help explain the authors' topic. Use a chart to list the details that support the authors' purpose for writing.

# Conclusions

Sometimes authors do not tell all the details. Readers can use text evidence in the words and pictures and think about what they already know to make a smart guess about what the author does not tell. This smart guess is a **conclusion.**

Think about the page in the selection that tells about honey. One conclusion you might make is that bees make honey from flower nectar.

# Your Turn

## RETURN TO THE ESSENTIAL QUESTION

**Turn and Talk**

**What do farmers need to grow food?** Think about what the authors want you to learn. Take turns asking questions about where food comes from. Use details and other text evidence to help you answer.

### Classroom Conversation

Talk about these questions with your class.

1. Where does apple juice come from? How do you think it is made?

2. How are trees important in this selection? How are animals important?

3. Why did the authors write this selection?

**WRITE ABOUT READING** ·····································

**Response** Write a paragraph about your favorite food from the selection. Begin with a topic sentence to tell which food is your favorite. Next, write detail sentences to tell why you like it. Give reasons. Then write a sentence that gives an ending.

My favorite food is

### Writing Tip

A closing sentence comes at the end. It gives your writing a nice ending.

# FAIRY TALE

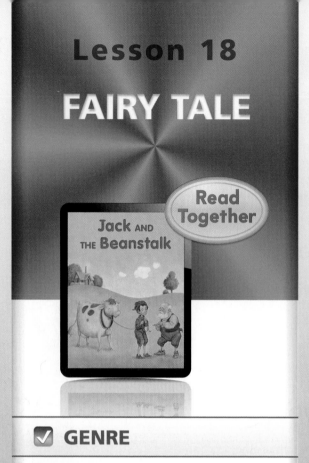

✓ **GENRE**

A **fairy tale** is an old story with characters that can do amazing things.

✓ **TEXT FOCUS**

Many fairy tales have **storytelling phrases**, such as **once upon a time** and **happily ever after**. Find these words. How do they make you feel? Why do you think the storyteller uses them?

# Jack AND THE Beanstalk

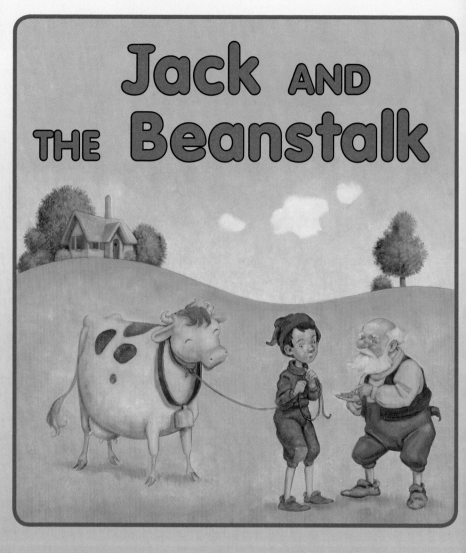

Once upon a time, there was a boy named Jack. He and his mom had no money for food because someone had taken their goose. Sometimes, it would lay golden eggs for them!

Jack went to sell their cow. He met a man. "I will trade these special beans for your cow," the man said.

Jack came home. His mother was mad. She threw the beans on the ground.

Soon a tall beanstalk grew. Jack climbed it. At the top was a huge castle. Inside, Jack found his goose in a cage under a table!

Then Jack heard, "FEE! FIE! FOE! FUM! Look out! Here I come!"

It was a giant! First Jack grabbed the goose. Then he ran right out the door.

Jack climbed down the beanstalk as fast as he could. He chopped it down.

Now Jack and his mother were safe, and they had their goose. They all lived happily ever after.

# Compare Texts

Read Together

## TEXT TO TEXT

**Write About Food** Choose three foods shown in the selections. Write sentences to tell where each food comes from. What else did you learn?

## TEXT TO SELF

**Tell About Food** Describe beans or another vegetable you have eaten. Tell how it looked and tasted.

## TEXT TO WORLD

**Connect to Technology** Use the Internet to find out how people grow a food you like. Draw a picture that shows what you learned.

# Grammar

Names of Months, Days, and Holidays

The names of **months** in a year, **days** of the week, and **holidays** begin with a capital letter. When you write a date, use a **comma** between the day of the month and the year.

Read Together

### Months
We planted seeds on May 14, 2018.

### Days of the Week
My dad cooked soup on Friday.

### Holidays
My family eats turkey on Thanksgiving.

Write each sentence correctly. Use another sheet of paper. Tell a partner what you did to correct each sentence.

1. Ali began school on september 8 2017.

2. She has science club every friday.

3. There was no school on memorial day.

4. Last wednesday our class took a field trip.

5. School ended on june 14 2018.

## Connect Grammar to Writing

When you proofread your writing, be sure you have written the names of months, days, and holidays correctly.

# Narrative Writing

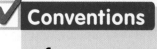 **Conventions** When you write a **friendly letter,** use different kinds of sentences to make it lively and interesting.

Ned drafted a letter about a special meal he had. Then he added a question.

**Revised Draft**

Then we tasted all the food.
Can you guess my favorite?
ᐱ The apple pie was best of all!

**Writing Checklist**

 **Conventions** Did I write different kinds of sentences?

✓ Did I tell about events in order?

✓ Did I use capital letters and commas correctly?

Look for different kinds of sentences in Ned's final copy. Then revise your writing. Use the Checklist.

**Final Copy**

March 8, 2018

Dear Mario,

My school had a potluck supper. First, each class cooked something. Then we tasted all the food. Can you guess my favorite? The apple pie was best of all!

Your friend,

Ned

Tomás Rivera
by Jane Medina
illustrated by René King Moreno

Life
Then and Now

---

## 🔍 LANGUAGE DETECTIVE

**Talk About Words**
Work with a partner. Choose one of the sentences on the **Context Cards.** Take out the yellow word. Put in a word that means the same or almost the same thing. Tell how the sentences are the same and different.

# Words to Know

Read Together

▶ Read each **Context Card.**

▶ Use a blue word to tell a story about a picture.

**1  work**

People go to work every day.

**2  great**

She did a great job baking this cake!

**3** **talk**

He likes to **talk** with customers at his job.

**4** **paper**

This artist does his work on **paper**.

**5** **were**

The farmers **were** very busy today.

**6** **soon**

**Soon** it will be time to go to lunch.

**7** **laugh**

A silly clown makes everyone **laugh**.

**8** **done**

He goes home when the work is **done**.

# Read and Comprehend

☑ **TARGET SKILL**

**Sequence of Events** The order of events in a selection is called the **sequence of events.** In many selections, the events are told in time order. As you read, think about what happens **first, next,** and **last.** You can use a flow chart to tell the order of events.

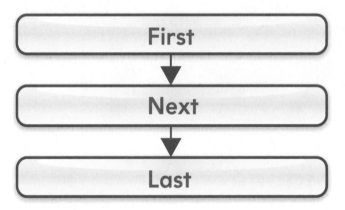

First

↓

Next

↓

Last

☑ **TARGET STRATEGY**

**Monitor/Clarify** If some parts or words don't make sense, you can ask questions, reread, and use the pictures for help.

## History

People did many things long ago that we still do today. They went to school. They worked. Families had fun.

Today we also do new things that people did not know about long ago. You will read about a boy and his Grandpa in **Tomás Rivera.**

### Talk About It

What do you do that your grandparents did not do as children? Write about it. Share your ideas with your classmates.

# ANCHOR TEXT

✅ **GENRE**

A **biography** tells about a person's life. As you read, look for:

▸ information about why the person is important

▸ events in time order

## Meet the Author

### Jane Medina

Jane Medina is both a teacher and a writer, just like Tomás Rivera. She began writing when she was a teenager. Since then, she has written books of poems in Spanish and English.

## Meet the Illustrator

### René King Moreno

As a young girl, René King Moreno loved to draw and paint. She also loved going to the library. She studied art in school, and now she illustrates children's books.

# Tomás Rivera

by Jane Medina

illustrated by
René King Moreno

**ESSENTIAL QUESTION**

Why is it important to
learn about people
from the past?

Tomás Rivera was born in Texas.
Tomás and his family went from
place to place picking crops.

Tomás helped pick crops all day. It was a lot of **work**. When the work was **done**, Tomás would **talk** with his Grandpa.

**ANALYZE THE TEXT**

**Sequence of Events** When do Grandpa and Tomás work? What happens after work?

"Come quick!" Grandpa called.
"It's time for stories!"

"You tell the best stories!"
Tomás said. "I wish I could
tell great stories, too."

The next day, Grandpa said, "We can get lots of stories for you, Tomás."
"When?" asked Tomás.

"Quick, hop in!" Grandpa said with a wink.
"I will show you!"
Grandpa drove the truck up the road.

"This is a library," said Grandpa.
"Look at all the books!" gasped Tomás.

"Read all you can, Tomás. It will help you think of lots of stories," said Grandpa.

There were lots of books for Tomás to read.
Some were funny and made him laugh. He
read about boats, trains, and cars. He
dreamed of space. Soon Tomás was thinking
of his own stories.

Tomás began telling his stories.
Then he wrote them on paper.

**ANALYZE THE TEXT**

**Using Context** How do the sentences and the picture help you know the word **paper**?

When he was a grown-up, Tomás got a
job as a teacher. He still wrote stories.

Tomás Rivera's stories tell about people
picking crops, just as his family did.
Lots of people read his books.

Now his name is on a big library.
Many people go to the library.
They get books, just as Tomás did.

# Dig Deeper

Read Together

## Use Clues to Analyze the Text

Use these pages to learn about Sequence of Events and Using Context. Then read **Tomás Rivera** again.

### Sequence of Events

**Tomás Rivera** tells about what happens to a real person. The order in which events happen is the **sequence of events.** When the story begins, Tomás is a child. What important events happen before Tomás becomes a writer? You can use a chart to show how events are connected.

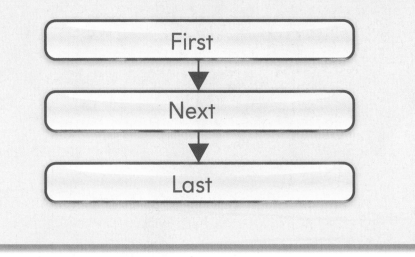

First

↓

Next

↓

Last

## Using Context

When you don't know what a word means, you can read the other words in the sentence to help you figure it out. You can also look at the pictures.

In the story, it says the family was picking **crops**. You can use the word **picking** and the picture of the farmer's field as text evidence to figure out that **crops** means "food that a farmer grows."

# Your Turn

## RETURN TO THE ESSENTIAL QUESTION

 **Why is it important to learn about people from the past?** Think about the selection. Take turns with your partner telling the events in order. Use text evidence. Add your ideas to what your partner says.

### 💬 Classroom Conversation

Now talk about these questions with your class.

1. How did Tomás get ideas for the stories he wrote?

2. What did Tomás learn from his Grandpa?

3. What did you learn about the past from this selection?

**WRITE ABOUT READING**

**Response** Write sentences that tell what Tomás is like. Begin with a sentence that tells your main idea. Next, write sentences to describe Tomás. Use facts and text evidence for ideas. Write a closing sentence.

### Writing Tip

A closing sentence comes at the end. It gives your writing a nice ending.

# INFORMATIONAL TEXT

**Read Together**

## ✓ GENRE

**Informational text** gives facts about a topic. This online encyclopedia entry was written to give true information.

## ✓ TEXT FOCUS

A **chart** is a drawing that lists information in a clear way. It can show words or pictures or both. What information do you learn from the chart on page 150?

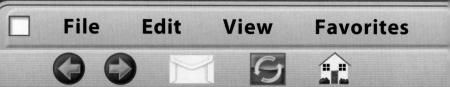

| | File | Edit | View | Favorites |

# Life
## Then and Now

The way people live changes over time. Today families live differently than in the past.

In the past, many jobs were done by hand. Now people have machines to help them do work.

In the past, people wrote letters on paper and sent them by mail. Now people can send messages right away. They talk on cell phones or send e-mails by computer.

In the past, families listened to radio programs. Now families watch TV programs and movies.

**Family Life**

We use many of the same kinds of things that people used in the past.

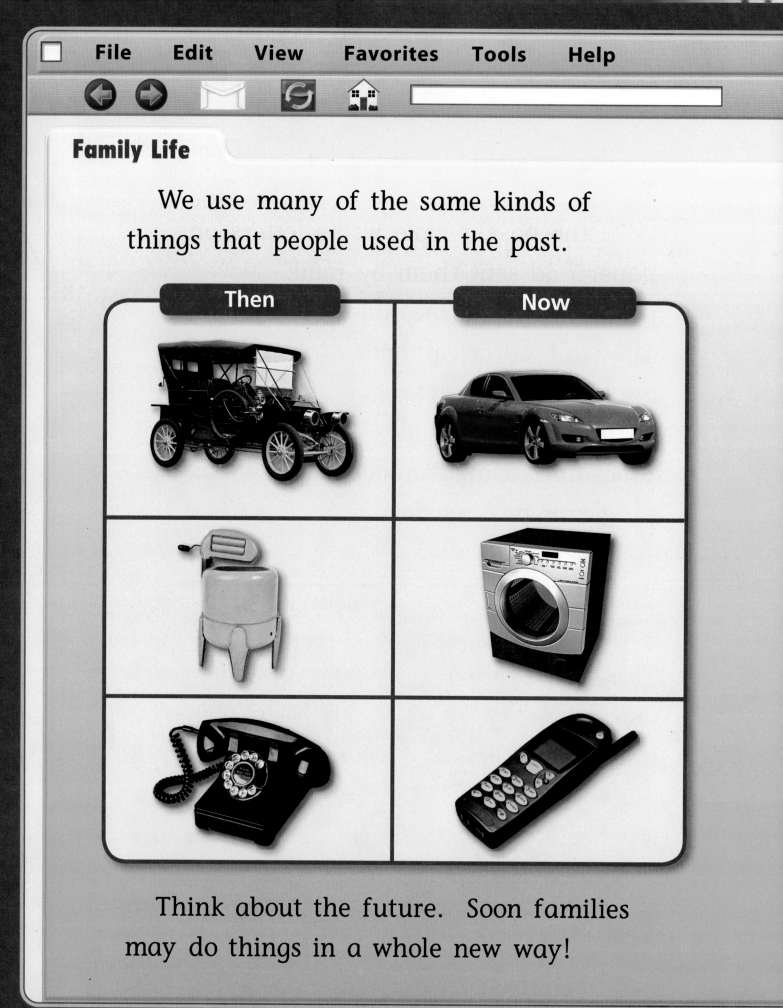

Then

Now

Think about the future.  Soon families may do things in a whole new way!

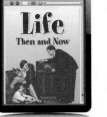

# Compare Texts

**Read Together**

## TEXT TO TEXT

**Recognize Purpose** Were the selections written to give information or to make you laugh? How do you know? What things did you learn?

## TEXT TO SELF

**Connect to Social Studies** Tell about a job you would like to have. Speak clearly and stay on topic.

## TEXT TO WORLD

**Think About It** What information did you learn from **Life Then and Now**? How has life changed? Do you think the new things are better? Tell why or why not.

# Grammar

**Verbs and Time** Verbs can tell what is happening now, in the past, or in the future. Verbs with **will** or **going to** tell about the future.

Read Together

| Now | In the Future |
|---|---|
| I read a book. | I will read a book. |
| Ana writes a story. | Ana is going to write a story. |

152

Read each sentence with a partner. Find the sentences that tell about the future. Then rewrite the other sentences to tell about the future. Use another sheet of paper.

1. I will go to the library.

2. I am going to find books.

3. I buy some books at the store.

4. My dad is going to read them to me.

5. I write a poem.

## Connect Grammar to Writing

When you revise your writing, you can use **will** or **going to** in sentences to tell about the future.

# Narrative Writing

✓ **Organization** Before you write a **personal narrative,** you need to plan what to say.

Read Together

Ava told her story to Zoe. That helped Ava choose events and details for her story.

**Exploring a Topic**

## Prewriting Checklist

 Did I choose an interesting topic?

 Are the events in my flow chart in order?

✓ Do my details tell who, what, where, and when?

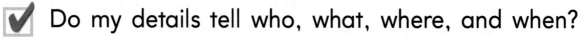

Look at the details Ava put in her chart. Plan your own story using a flow chart. Write sentences or notes in order to tell about events. Use the Checklist.

## Planning Chart

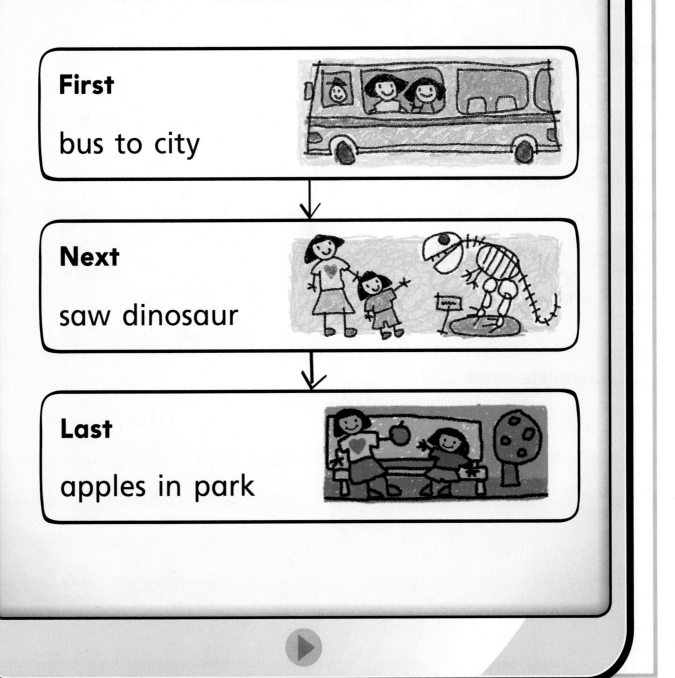

**First**

bus to city

**Next**

saw dinosaur

**Last**

apples in park

## 🔍 LANGUAGE DETECTIVE

**Talk About Words**
Work with a partner. Choose your favorite photo. Tell why it's your favorite. Use as many of the blue words as possible. Be sure to use complete sentences.

# Words to Know

▶ Read each **Context Card**.

▶ Use a blue word to tell about something you did.

**1** **want**
They **want** to pick apples today.

**2** **old**
This little apple tree is not very **old**.

**3 try**

They try to find the best apples.

**4 use**

Use a ladder to reach the high apples.

**5 more**

No more apples will fit in here!

**6 wash**

Be sure to wash the apples.

**7 mother**

Ben's mother helps us make a pie.

**8 door**

Open the oven door when the pie is done.

door

# Read and Comprehend

✓ **TARGET SKILL**

**Cause and Effect** Sometimes one event makes another event happen. The **cause** happens first. It is the reason why something else happens. The **effect** is what happens next. As you read, ask yourself what happens and why. Use a chart like this one to help you understand causes and effects.

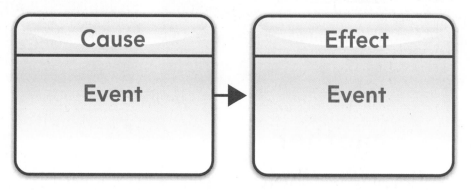

| Cause | Effect |
|-------|--------|
| Event | Event |

✓ **TARGET STRATEGY**

**Infer/Predict** Use text evidence to figure out more and what might happen next.

## Feelings

When someone tells a joke, you laugh. When a friend moves away, you are sad. When something scary happens, you may get frightened. We show feelings in many different ways.

You will read about what happens when Little Rabbit gets scared in **Little Rabbit's Tale.**

💬 **Think | Draw | Pair | Share**

Who can help you feel better when you feel sad? Think about it. Draw a picture. Show your picture as you talk to help explain your answer to a partner.

159

# ANCHOR TEXT

Little Rabbit's Tale

by Wong Herbert Yee
illustrated by Richard Bernal

## ✓ GENRE

A **folktale** is an old story told for many years. Look for:

▶ a lesson about life
▶ animals who act like people
▶ the words **happily ever after**

**Meet the Author**

## Wong Herbert Yee

Wong Herbert Yee loves to write and draw. "Little Rabbit reminds me of my daughter Ellen," he says. "Her favorite animal is a rabbit. I try to put a rabbit in every story I write!"

**Meet the Illustrator**

## Richard Bernal

Richard Bernal started drawing when he was in the first grade. He says, "I like to have fun when I make pictures. See if you can find the letters **r.b.** marked on a tree!"

# Little Rabbit's Tale

by Wong Herbert Yee
illustrated by Richard Bernal

**ESSENTIAL QUESTION**

How can you help a
friend who feels sad?

Little Rabbit sleeps under an old apple
tree.   Just then, the wind starts to blow.
The branches shift in the wind.

Something hits Little Rabbit.

**ANALYZE THE TEXT**

**Cause and Effect** What causes
Little Rabbit to wake up?

"Oh, no! The sky is falling!" yells
Little Rabbit. "I've got to try to
tell everyone!"
Little Rabbit hops off to find Goose.

Goose sits in his rowboat.
The tip of his rod starts to twitch.
"There's no time to fish!" yells
Little Rabbit.  "The sky is falling!"

"Let's go, Little Rabbit! We need to go tell Beaver!"
Goose and Little Rabbit use the rowboat.
They go up the stream.

Goose peeks inside.

Beaver is eating a snack.

"There's no time to eat," says Goose.

"Let's go! The sky is falling!"

"Oh my!" says Beaver. "We need
to go tell Turtle."
Beaver, Goose, and Little Rabbit
dash up the hill.

Turtle sleeps under a log.
TAP, TAP! Beaver taps on Turtle's shell. Turtle peeks out.
"There's no time to sleep," says Beaver.
"Let's go! The sky is falling!"

"Oh, no!" yells Turtle. "What can we do?"
"Let's run back home," says Little Rabbit.
"I want to tell my mother!"

Turtle, Beaver, Goose, and Little Rabbit
run fast.  They hop over the log,
dash down the hill, . . .

and jump into Goose's rowboat.
Then they go as fast as they can
down the stream.

Little Rabbit hops in the door.
"Mother, the sky is falling!"
"Who told you such a thing?"
asks Mother Rabbit.

"Beaver told me!" says Turtle.
"Goose told me!" says Beaver.
"Little Rabbit told me!" says Goose.
"Well let's just go outside and look
at the sky," says Mother Rabbit.

Just then, the wind starts to blow.
The branches shift in the wind.

# Thump!

Something hits Little Rabbit.

**ANALYZE THE TEXT**

**Story Lesson** What lesson do you think the characters learn on this page?

"Oh, no! The sky is falling!" yells Little Rabbit.

"The sky is not falling," laughs Mother Rabbit. "An apple just fell from the apple tree!"

"I didn't get to catch a fish," says Goose.
"I didn't get to eat my snack," says Beaver.
"I didn't get to sleep," says Turtle.

"I've got a plan," says Little Rabbit.
"Can my friends eat with us?"
"Yes," says Mother Rabbit.  "Go wash
your hands while I get more plates."

Little Rabbit has a nice meal with
his friends.  After that, they all
have homemade apple treats!

*The friends lived happily ever after!*

# Dig Deeper

## Use Clues to Analyze the Text

Use these pages to learn about Cause and Effect and Story Lesson. Then read **Little Rabbit's Tale** again.

## Cause and Effect

In **Little Rabbit's Tale**, Little Rabbit gets hit on the head. This is the **cause** that makes something else happen. What happens next because he got hit? This is the **effect**. As you read, think about what happens and why. You can use a chart to show other causes and effects.

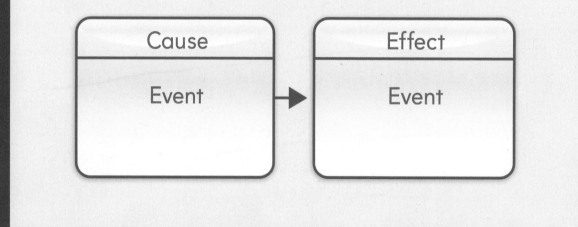

| Cause | | Effect |
|-------|---|--------|
| Event | → | Event |

## Story Lesson

**Little Rabbit's Tale** is a folktale. Have you ever heard a story that sounds like this one? People told a story like this for many years before it was written down.

Folktales often have an important message. The message of the story is a lesson about life. What can you learn from **Little Rabbit's Tale**?

# Your Turn

## RETURN TO THE ESSENTIAL QUESTION

 **How can you help a friend who feels sad?** How do Little Rabbit's mother and friends help him? What things make this a funny story? Use text evidence such as words and pictures to answer.

### 💬 Classroom Conversation

Talk about these questions with your class.

1. Why do you think Little Rabbit acts the way he does when an apple falls on him?

2. What happens over and over in this story?

3. Why are the friends happy at the end?

182

### WRITE ABOUT READING ··································

**Response** Write a letter to Little Rabbit. Tell him how you think he should have acted. First, talk to a partner about your ideas. Then use some of your partner's ideas and your own ideas to make your writing better.

**Writing Tip**

A letter starts with a greeting like this.
**Dear Little Rabbit,**

# POETRY

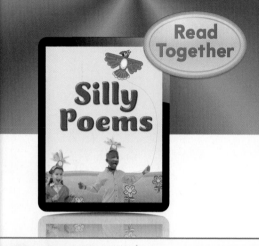

Read Together

Silly Poems

## ☑ GENRE

**Poetry** uses the sounds of words to show pictures and feelings. Some poems use rhyming words and other patterns to make them fun to read.

## ☑ TEXT FOCUS

**Rhythm** is a pattern of beats in a poem. Sometimes you can clap along with the rhythm of a poem. Try clapping along with the poems in this selection.

### Readers' Theater

# Silly Poems

**READER 1** What do you want to do when you grow up?

**READER 2** I want to fly like a bird!

**BOTH** Let's try reading this flying poem together.

# Wouldn't You?

If I
Could go
As high
And low
As the wind
As the wind
As the wind
Can blow —

I'd go!

*by John Ciardi*

**READER 1**  Let's read another poem!

**READER 2**  Who is more afraid, the elephant or the mouse?  I'll read the first four lines.  You read the rest.

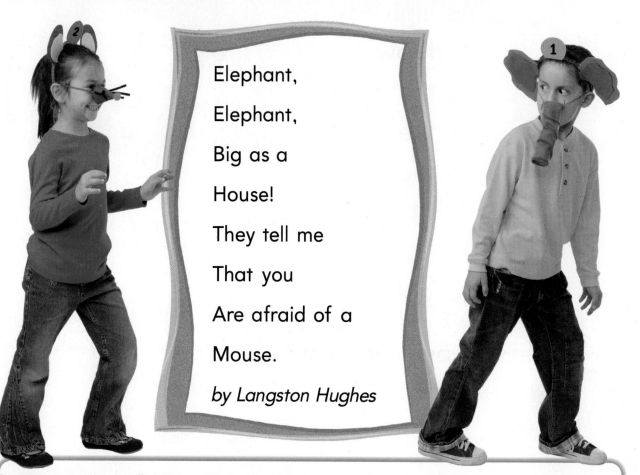

Elephant,

Elephant,

Big as a

House!

They tell me

That you

Are afraid of a

Mouse.

*by Langston Hughes*

## Respond to Poetry

• Write a silly poem.  Use rhyming and feeling words.  Use words that tell what things look like or sound like.  Read your poem aloud.

• Choose a poem or rhyme to memorize.  Say it aloud to a partner.  Use your voice to show how it makes you feel.

# Compare Texts

**Read Together**

## TEXT TO TEXT

**Talk About It** Talk with a partner about the silly things Little Rabbit does. What is silly about the poems? Take turns talking.

## TEXT TO SELF

**Write Silly Sentences** Write sentences to tell classmates about something silly that you saw or did.

## TEXT TO WORLD

**Connect to Social Studies** Find out where apples grow. Use the symbols on a map. Tell what you find out, using words like **north**, **south**, **east**, or **west**.

# Grammar

**Prepositions** A **preposition** is a word that joins with other words to help explain where something is or when it happens. A **prepositional phrase** is a group of words that starts with a preposition.

Read Together

The rabbit napped <u>under</u> a tree.
He napped <u>before</u> the apple fell.
The apples are <u>on</u> the branch.

**Try This!**

Read each sentence with a partner. Find the preposition and prepositional phrase in each sentence. Write them on another sheet of paper. Talk with your partner to decide whether the preposition tells where or when something happened.

1. Ted read a book before dinner.

2. He was in an apple tree.

3. There was a sound above his head.

4. A bird flew around him.

5. He was right by its nest!

## Connect Grammar to Writing

When you revise your writing, be sure to include prepositional phrases to tell where and when.

# Narrative Writing

✔️ **Development**  In a good **personal narrative,** exact details help readers picture the events that happened.

Ava wrote about a special day. Later, she changed words to make them more exact.

**Read Together**

## Revised Draft

Then we went to a museum.
I saw ~~stuff.~~ rocks, stars, and dinosaurs.

## Revising Checklist

 Do my sentences have exact details?

 Did I use time-order words?

 Did I write a sentence that tells the end of the story?

190

**Final Copy**

# A Great Day

Last Friday, my mom and I had an adventure. First, we took a bus to the city. Then we went to a museum. I saw rocks, stars, and dinosaurs. Last, we ate some apples in the park. I hope we have another great day soon!

# Write a Book Report

Read
Together

**TASK** Look at **The Big Trip.** Do you like this story? Think about how you feel about it. Write a book report to tell classmates your opinion of **The Big Trip.**

**PLAN** 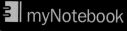 myNotebook

**Gather Information** Talk with a group about **The Big Trip.** Tell about parts you like or don't like. Use words and pictures in the story to help you tell why.

Use the tools in your eBook to remember important details from **The Big Trip.**

Write your ideas on a chart.

- What is your opinion of the whole story? Do you like it or not?

- What are two good reasons for your opinion?

- Find examples in the story to explain your reasons.

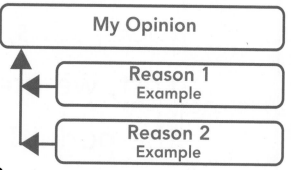

My Opinion

Reason 1
Example

Reason 2
Example

Write your
draft in
*my*WriteSmart.

## Write Your Book Report  Use your chart for ideas.  Follow these steps.

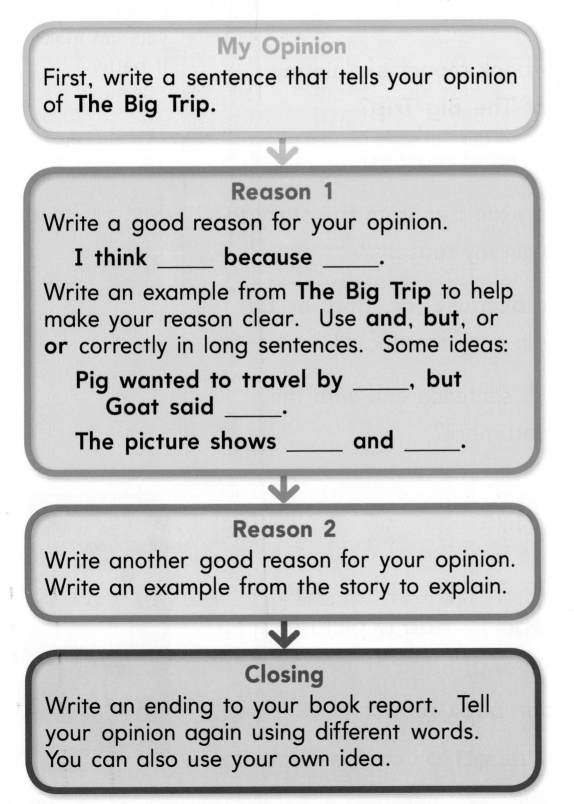

**My Opinion**

First, write a sentence that tells your opinion of **The Big Trip.**

**Reason 1**

Write a good reason for your opinion.

  **I think _____ because _____.**

Write an example from **The Big Trip** to help make your reason clear.  Use **and**, **but**, or **or** correctly in long sentences.  Some ideas:

  **Pig wanted to travel by _____, but
    Goat said _____.**

  **The picture shows _____ and _____.**

**Reason 2**

Write another good reason for your opinion. Write an example from the story to explain.

**Closing**

Write an ending to your book report. Tell your opinion again using different words. You can also use your own idea.

**Review Your Draft**   Read your writing and make it better.  Use the Checklist.

Ask a partner to read your draft. Talk about how you can make it better.

  Does my book report explain my opinion of **The Big Trip?**

  Did I give good reasons?

  Did I use examples from the story to help explain my reasons?

  Did I use **because**, **or**, **and**, or **but** correctly in long sentences?

  Does each sentence end with the correct end mark?

 **PRESENT**

**Share**   Write or type a final copy of your book report.  Add a picture. Pick a way to share.

- Read your book report to a group.

- Put your report on a class website.

## Unit 4   High-Frequency Words

**16 Let's Go to the Moon!**

| | |
|---|---|
| think | because |
| bring | carry |
| before | show |
| light | around |

**17 The Big Trip**

| | |
|---|---|
| there | don't |
| by | car |
| sure | about |
| could | maybe |

**18 Where Does Food Come From?**

| | |
|---|---|
| food | under |
| first | these |
| ground | right |
| sometimes | your |

**19 Tomás Rivera**

| | |
|---|---|
| work | were |
| great | soon |
| talk | laugh |
| paper | done |

**20 Little Rabbit's Tale**

| | |
|---|---|
| want | more |
| old | wash |
| try | mother |
| use | door |

# Glossary

## A

**apple**
An **apple** is a fruit with red, yellow, or green skin.
José picked a red **apple** from that tree.

## B

**beaver**
A **beaver** is an animal that has large front teeth and a flat tail. We saw a **beaver** swimming in the water.

**born**
**Born** means brought to life. The kittens were **born** yesterday.

# C

**chocolate**

**Chocolate** is a kind of food that is dark and sweet.
**Chocolate** is my favorite kind of candy.

**crater**

A **crater** is a large hole in the ground. We saw
a picture of a big **crater** on the Moon.

# D

**desert**

A **desert** is a large dry area of land.
The **desert** has a lot of sand.

# E

**engine**

An **engine** is a kind of machine that
burns oil, gas, or wood. My sister's
car has an **engine** that makes it go
very fast.

**exclaimed**

To **exclaim** means to say something in a strong way.
"Watch out!" Dillon **exclaimed**.

# F

**family**

A **family** is a group of people who often live together.
Our **family** lives in the city.

**favorite**

**Favorite** means what you like the most.
My **favorite** pet is a dog.

**footprints**

A **footprint** is the mark
a person or an animal
leaves. We looked back
and saw our **footprints** in
the sand.

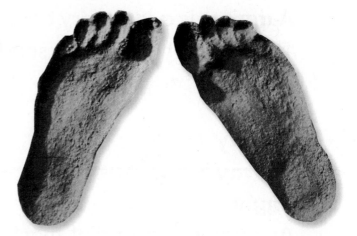

# G

**goose**
A **goose** is a kind of bird that has a long neck.
The **goose** is sitting on her nest.

**gravity**
**Gravity** is the force that pulls us to the ground.
**Gravity** is stronger on Earth than it is on the Moon.

# H

**happily ever after**
**Happily ever after** is a storytelling phrase that
means happy from that time on. The three little
pigs lived **happily ever after**.

**hooray**
**Hooray** is a word that people shout when they are
happy. When Jim won the race, we yelled, "**Hooray!**"

# I

**island**
An **island** is an area of land that has water all around it.
Risa and her family took a boat to the **island**.

# J

## jumpy

**Jumpy** means moving in a way that isn't smooth. Tino moved in a **jumpy** way that made him spill his milk.

# L

## library

A **library** is a place where books are kept. I borrow a book from the **library** each Monday.

## lunar

**Lunar** means having to do with the Moon. My grandpa remembers watching the first **lunar** landing on TV.

# O

## oh

**Oh** is a word that shows strong feelings. "**Oh** no!" said Mom when the car did not start.

# P

**paddies**

A **paddy** is a field of rice. The people worked hard in the rice **paddies**.

**parachute**

When you **parachute**, you use something that opens up and helps you float to the ground. After he jumps from the plane, Elliott will **parachute** to the ground.

**people**

**People** means more than one person. Lots of **people** came to hear Ben sing.

# R

**rabbit**

A **rabbit** is an animal with long ears and soft fur. My pet **rabbit** likes to hop.

**rocket**

A **rocket** is something that flies in space. A hundred years ago, no one believed we would send a **rocket** to the Moon.

**rover**

A **rover** is something that moves from one place to another. The **rover** moved across the Moon's surface.

# S

**says**

**Says** means tells. Mom **says** that Dad will be home soon.

**sky**

The **sky** is the air above the ground. I saw a plane fly high in the **sky**.

**stories**

A **story** is writing that tells what happens to people or to other characters. My grandma tells **stories** about what she did when she was a girl.

**stubborn**

If you are **stubborn**, that means you don't change your mind easily. My little sister can be **stubborn** when she wants her way.

# T

**teacher**

A **teacher** is a person who teaches others. My mother is a math **teacher**.

**Texas**

**Texas** is a state in the United States of America. We like to visit our grandpa in **Texas**.

**told**

**Told** means said something to someone. My friend **told** me a funny joke today.

**Tomás Rivera**

**Tomás Rivera** was a writer and a teacher. **Tomás Rivera** began writing when he was a young boy.

**travel**

To **travel** means to go and visit another place. Next summer we are going to **travel** to South America.

**troubles**

**Trouble** is something that makes it hard to know what to do. That place has had many **troubles** over the years.

## tunnel

A **tunnel** goes under ground or water to help people get from one place to another. They drove through a **tunnel** to get to the city.

## V

## vegetables

A **vegetable** is a plant or a part of a plant that you can eat. You should eat **vegetables** because they are good for you.

# Acknowledgments

*The Big Trip* written and illustrated by Valeri Gorbachev. Copyright ©2004 by Valeri Gorbachev. Reprinted by permission of Philomel Books, a Division of Penguin Young Readers Group, a member of Penguin Group (USA) Inc. All rights reserved.

"Elephant, Elephant" from *The Sweet and Sour Animal Book* by Langston Hughes. Copyright ©1994 by Ramona Bass and Arnold Rampersad, Administrators of the Estate of Langston Hughes. Reprinted by permission of Oxford University Press and Harold Ober Associates, Inc.

*Where Does Food Come From?* by Shelley Rotner and Gary Goss, photographs by Shelley Rotner. Text copyright ©2006 by Shelley Rotner and Gary Goss. Photographs copyright ©2006 by Shelley Rotner. Reprinted by permission of Millbrook Press, a division of Lerner Publishing Group. All rights reserved.

"Wouldn't You?" from *You Read to Me, I'll Read to You* by John Ciardi. Text copyright ©1961 by John Ciardi. Reprinted by permission of HarperCollins Publishers.

# Credits

## Placement Key:
(r) right, (l) left, (c) center, (t) top, (b) bottom, (bg) background

## Photo Credits
**3** (b) ©Dennis Hallinan/Alamy Images; **3** (b) ©NASA; **3** (cl) ©Stockbyte/Getty Images; **3** (cl) ©NASA Marshall Space Flight Center; **4** (bl) ©Montana Historical Society; **4** (bl) ©Montana Historical Society; **6** (tl) ©Camerique Archive/ Getty Images; ©Les Gibbon/Alamy Images;**8** ©PatrikOntkovic/Shutterstock; Blind [**9**] ©Jupiterimages/Getty Images; **10** (tl) ©Dennis Hallinan/Alamy Images; **10** (tc) ©NASA; **10** (t) ©JUPITERIMAGES/ BananaStock/Alamy; **10** (b) ©NASA/Handout/Getty Images News/ Getty Images North America/Getty Images; **10** (tc) ©Stockbyte/Getty Images; **11** (cr) ©NASA; **11** (tl) ©Maxim Marmur/AFP/Getty Images; **11** (tr) ©Corbis; **11** (cl) ©NASA/CORBIS; **11** (bl) ©Sean Sexton Collection/Corbis; **11** (br) ©NASA/Corbis; **12** © Clearviewstock / Alamy; **12** ©Dennis Hallinan/Alamy Images; **13** ©Corbis; **14** (tl) ©Dennis Hallinan/Alamy Images; **15** ©Dennis Hallinan/Alamy Images; **16** ©Science Source/ Photo Researchers, Inc.; **18** ©NASA; **19** ©NASA/ Science Source/Photo Researchers; **20** ©NASA/ Stringer/Time & Life Pictures/Getty Images; **21** ©NASA/Photo Researchers, Inc.; **22** ©Keystone/ Stringer/Getty Images; **24** ©NASA; **25** © MPI/ Stringer/Hulton Archive/Getty Images; **26** ©NASA; **28** ©NASA; **29** ©NASA; **30** ©NASA; **31** ©CORBIS; **32** ©Brand X/SuperStock; **34** ©Robert Karpa/Masterfile; **36** (tl) ©Dennis Hallinan/Alamy Images; **37** (b) ©CORBIS; **38** ©HMH; **39** (tl) ©Dennis Hallinan/Alamy Images; **39** (c) StockTrek/Photodisc/Getty Images; **40** ©NASA Marshall Space Flight Center; **40** (tl) ©Stockbyte/Getty Images; **40** (tl) ©NASA Marshall Space Flight Center; **42** (tl) ©Bettmann/ Corbis; **42** (b) ©Time Life Pictures/Getty Images; **42** (b) ©Robert Mora/Getty Entertainment/ Getty Images; **42** ©Stockbyte/Getty Images; **43** (c) Dmitriy Shironosov / Alamy; **43** (t) NASA; **43** (b) © Purestock/SuperStock; **43** (tc) ©Stockbyte/ Getty Images; **43** (tl) ©NASA Marshall Space Flight Center; **43** (tl) ©Dennis Hallinan/Alamy Images; **44** (b) ©PhotoDisc; **45** (cr) ©World Perspectives/Getty Images; **48** (b) Tony Freeman/

Houghton
Mifflin
Harcourt

# NATIONAL
# JOURNEYS

**Program Consultants**

Shervaughnna Anderson · Marty Hougen

Carol Jago · Erik Palmer · Shane Templeton

Sheila Valencia · MaryEllen Vogt

**Consulting Author** · Irene Fountas

## Unit 4

# Exploring Together .................... 9

**Lesson**

**18**

TOPIC: **Agriculture**

## Amazing Whales!

INFORMATIONAL TEXT

by Sarah L. Thomson

# Be a Reading Detective!

## Welcome, Reader!

Your help is needed to find clues in texts. As a **Reading Detective**, you will need to **ask lots of questions.** You will also need to **read carefully.**

### myNotebook

As you read, mark up the text. Save your work to **myNotebook**.

- Highlight details.
- Add notes and questions.
- Add new words to **myWordList**.

- Use letters and sounds you know to help you read the words.

- Look at the pictures.

- Think about what is happening.

**Let's go!**

# Exploring Together

**Stream to Start**

> 66 Can't keep still all day...
> I like adventure, and I'm going to find one. 99
> — Louisa May Alcott

## Performance Task Preview

At the end of this unit, you will write a book report about a story you read. You will use details from the story to tell what you think of it.

hmhfyi.com

Channel One News®

# 16

Let's Go to the Moon!
written by Stephen R. Swinburne

Mae Jemison

## 🔍 LANGUAGE DETECTIVE

**Talk About Words**
**Verbs** are words that tell what people and animals do. Work with a partner. Find the blue words that are verbs. Use them in complete sentences.

**▤ myNotebook**

Add new words to **myWordList**. Use them in your speaking and writing.

# Words to Know

Read Together

▶ Read each **Context Card**.

▶ Choose two blue words. Use them in sentences.

---

**1** **think**

What do you think space is like?

---

**2** **bring**

Spaceships can bring astronauts to space.

### 3 before

Astronauts practice flying **before** their trip.

### 4 light

People feel very **light** floating in space.

### 5 because

Astronauts like to jump **because** it is fun!

### 6 carry

Astronauts **carry** tools to work with.

### 7 show

Pictures **show** us what the Moon is like.

### 8 around

You can see clouds all **around** Earth.

# Read and Comprehend

☑ **TARGET SKILL**

**Main Idea and Details** The **topic** is the one big idea that the whole selection is about. The **main idea** is the most important idea about the topic. As you read, think about the **details**, or facts, that tell more about the main idea. You can list the main idea and details about the topic on a web.

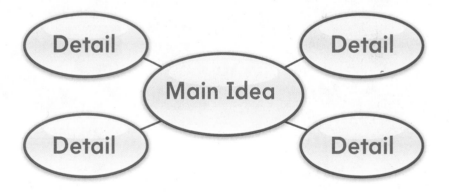

☑ **TARGET STRATEGY**

**Question** Ask questions about what you read. Look for text evidence to answer.

## Astronauts

Astronauts travel into space. Before they go, they plan what to bring. They have to bring food to last the whole trip. They also bring tools that help them work in space. They bring cameras to show people back on Earth what space looks like. You will read more about astronauts in **Let's Go to the Moon!**

### Think | Pair | Share

Would you like to go to the Moon? Why? Think about it. Complete the sentence: I would like to go to the Moon because ____. Share your answer.

# ANCHOR TEXT

Let's Go to the Moon!
written by Stephen R. Swinburne

**Informational text** gives facts about a topic. As you read, look for:
▸ words that tell facts
▸ photos that show the real world

**Meet the Author**

## Stephen R. Swinburne

Steve Swinburne has never been to the Moon, but he loves to travel and explore new places here on Earth. His trips have brought him close to bears, bobcats, and wolves! He has written many books about the things he has seen.

# Let's Go to the Moon!

written by Stephen R. Swinburne

**ESSENTIAL QUESTION**

What do astronauts do?

# Blast Off!

Would you like to fly to the Moon?  Let's go!